This Journal
Belongs To:

_____

Introduction

WRITING IS A FORM OF self-care. And out of lots of different self-care activities, writing or journaling is perhaps the most time and cost-effective one. Many studies have shown journaling helps manage stress, anxiety, and depression. Through gaining control of your emotions and having a better look at the situations and conditions in your life, you can work on reducing anxiety and ultimately improve your mental health.

Five to ten minutes of journaling daily can make a huge difference in case you been holding back bottled up emotions. The act of writing gives you an opportunity to step back from your feelings and thoughts and observe them as they are. It creates a medium for self-discovery and self-awareness. By allowing you to look at things as they are, you can get a deeper understanding of your strengths, goals, positive traits or things that you'd like to work on rather than focusing negative things that happened in the past or worrying about things in the future.

This journal has 100 therapeutic prompts that will encourage you to focus on the present and focus on the positive. By answering the prompts, you'll be focusing deep inside your psyche. The writing prompts in this journal are carefully chosen to encourage you to ponder about the positive things in your life and stay in the moment while being an observer of the things in your life. The writing prompts in this journal are also curated to keep you mindful rather than letting your mind cluttered with worries, fears or negative thoughts.

Through the end of this journal, you'll notice that you'll be staying in the moment more rather than focusing on negative thoughts, worries or bodily sensations. And you'll find the amazing beauty in the disarray of your real life by focusing on your strengths, connections, positive traits and goals in life.

As a form of therapeutic expression, many have gained comparable results with regular talk therapy. Journaling can lead to a reduced need for talk therapy for you as you keep using it as an expressive therapy.

Please keep in mind that journaling shouldn't replace other treatments or therapeutic practices you already use (if any), although there are many mental health benefits of journaling as a self-care activity.

Let's start with listing 5 things you're thankful for:

_____

_____

_____

_____

_____

_____

_____

_____

_____

_____

_____

_____

_____

_____

_____

_____

Write 3 things you're looking forward to this week:

Describe a situation where everything worked out fine for you:

Think of your victories this week and write
how you felt about them:

_____

_____

_____

_____

_____

_____

_____

_____

_____

_____

_____

_____

_____

_____

_____

_____

_____

Write a few words you'd like to hear right now:

Write about the kindest things anyone has ever said to you. And describe how you felt:

List 3 of your physical features you like or get compliments for:

Write a thank you letter to your body:

Remember one of your biggest accomplishments in life. Describe why it means so much to you:

_____

_____

_____

_____

_____

_____

_____

_____

_____

_____

_____

_____

_____

_____

_____

_____

_____

_____

_____

Complete the following sentence and explain why you would do that: If I didn't have any fear, I would_____

Think of your biggest supporter in life. And write a short thank you note to that person:

_____

_____

_____

_____

_____

_____

_____

_____

_____

_____

_____

_____

_____

_____

_____

_____

_____

Write about the positive changes you have made in the past year:

List 5 things you'd like to achieve this year:

List 3 songs that change your mood every
time you hear. And write the part of the
lyrics you like the most:

_____

_____

_____

_____

_____

_____

_____

_____

_____

_____

_____

_____

_____

_____

_____

_____

_____

_____

_____

Write about one thing you look forward to everyday:

Write about one thing you want people know about you and explain why:

_____

_____

_____

_____

_____

_____

_____

_____

_____

_____

_____

_____

_____

_____

_____

_____

Write 5 things/memories you forgive yourself for:

List 10 things that make you smile:

Write about 3 of your best talents:

Write about you favorite memory of all times:

_____

_____

_____

_____

_____

_____

_____

_____

_____

_____

_____

_____

_____

_____

_____

_____

_____

_____

Describe the kindest thing you can do for yourself right now:

List the things you believe you deserve in your life:

_____

_____

_____

_____

_____

_____

_____

_____

_____

_____

_____

_____

_____

_____

_____

_____

_____

_____

Write about the one thing that brings the most joy to you:

Write about why you deserve the best in life:

_____

_____

_____

_____

_____

_____

_____

_____

_____

_____

_____

_____

_____

_____

_____

_____

_____

_____

_____

List 3 of your past fears and write how you conquered them:

Write about your role model in life and
describe the things you like in that person:

_____

_____

_____

_____

_____

_____

_____

_____

_____

_____

_____

_____

_____

_____

_____

_____

_____

_____

_____

List 5 things you like about your personal style:

Write about an event that you believe made you stronger:

_____

_____

_____

_____

_____

_____

_____

_____

_____

_____

_____

_____

_____

_____

_____

_____

_____

_____

Think of a really peaceful moment in your
life and write about how it made you feel:

Write about love and describe what it means to you:

List 5 things you're proud of in your life:

Write about one lesson you learned in life so far:

Write your personal mission statement. If you don't have one, this is a good time to write one!:

_____

_____

_____

_____

_____

_____

_____

_____

_____

_____

_____

_____

_____

_____

_____

_____

_____

_____

Write about the ways you can love yourself today:

_____

_____

_____

_____

_____

_____

_____

_____

_____

_____

_____

_____

_____

_____

_____

_____

_____

_____

List 5 things you would love to learn:

Write about the lessons you learned from a book you've read recently:

_____

_____

_____

_____

_____

_____

_____

_____

_____

_____

_____

_____

_____

_____

_____

_____

_____

_____

Write about a big decision that frightened you initially but paid off in the end:

Describe how you'd like to change the way you respond to setbacks or failures:

_____

_____

_____

_____

_____

_____

_____

_____

_____

_____

_____

_____

_____

_____

_____

_____

_____

_____

_____

Write about 3 life lessons you'd like someone else to learn from you:

_____

_____

_____

_____

_____

_____

_____

_____

_____

_____

_____

_____

_____

_____

_____

_____

_____

_____

List some of the priorities you have in life right now:

_____

_____

_____

_____

_____

_____

_____

_____

_____

_____

_____

_____

_____

_____

_____

_____

_____

_____

Write about and obstacle you overcame this week:

Write a few beliefs you'd like to leave behind because they no longer serve your highest good:

_____

_____

_____

_____

_____

_____

_____

_____

_____

_____

_____

_____

_____

_____

_____

_____

_____

_____

Write about the present moment. Describe how you feel:

List 5 things you'd like to let go this year:

Write about a moment you felt
embarrassed but now you can look back
on and laugh about:

List your favorite TV shows and favorite characters in those shows:

_____

_____

_____

_____

_____

_____

_____

_____

_____

_____

_____

_____

_____

_____

_____

_____

_____

_____

_____

_____

_____

Write yourself 5 compliments:

_____

_____

_____

_____

_____

_____

_____

_____

_____

_____

_____

_____

_____

_____

_____

_____

_____

_____

Think of the smallest things that make you
happy and write about them:

_____

_____

_____

_____

_____

_____

_____

_____

_____

_____

_____

_____

_____

_____

_____

_____

_____

_____

_____

Write about your favorite city and describe what you love about that city:

Think of the most valuable friendship you've ever had in your life. And write 5 thinks you're grateful about it:

_____

_____

_____

_____

_____

_____

_____

_____

_____

_____

_____

_____

_____

_____

_____

_____

_____

_____

_____

List a few things you would like to improve on:

_____

_____

_____

_____

_____

_____

_____

_____

_____

_____

_____

_____

_____

_____

_____

_____

Write your favorite quote that inspires you everyday:

Use this page to free style about your
current thoughts and let yourself observe
the feelings they cause:

List your overall positive qualities:

Write about what makes you laugh and when was the last time you had a belly laugh:

List 5 of your goals for the next 5 years:

Write about the things you like to explore in life:

Think of an advice you'd give your younger self. And explain why:

_____

_____

_____

_____

_____

_____

_____

_____

_____

_____

_____

_____

_____

_____

_____

_____

_____

_____

Write about things that make you relax:

Write about the highs of this month. Also think about the lows and write about how you can learn from them:

Write about your favorite memory with your parents and/or siblings:

_____

_____

_____

_____

_____

_____

_____

_____

_____

_____

_____

_____

_____

_____

_____

_____

_____

Write about the 3 things you love about your significant other. If you haven't one right now, write about your ideal partner:

List your favorite sights of where you live in right now:

_____

_____

_____

_____

_____

_____

_____

_____

_____

_____

_____

_____

_____

_____

_____

_____

_____

_____

Write about the people you admire and explain why:

_____

_____

_____

_____

_____

_____

_____

_____

_____

_____

_____

_____

_____

_____

_____

_____

_____

_____

_____

_____

_____

_____

Think of all the things going well in your life right now and write about them:

_____

_____

_____

_____

_____

_____

_____

_____

_____

_____

_____

_____

_____

_____

_____

_____

_____

_____

Write how you've grown over the last two years:

_____

_____

_____

_____

_____

_____

_____

_____

_____

_____

_____

_____

_____

_____

_____

_____

_____

_____

Write about one thing you would do if you knew you could not fail:

Think of an imaginary phone conversation with someone and write what you'd tell that person on your current feelings:

Think of 3 things you'd prefer to do less of and write about the ways you can eliminate those things from your life:

Write about a few things holding you back in life and think of ways to work on those things:

List 3 things you want to try in the following years:

_____

_____

_____

_____

_____

_____

_____

_____

_____

_____

_____

_____

_____

_____

_____

_____

_____

_____

_____

Write about a lesson you learned from a challenge last year:

_____

_____

_____

_____

_____

_____

_____

_____

_____

_____

_____

_____

_____

_____

_____

_____

_____

_____

_____

Describe your favorite spot in your home
and write about how it makes you feel
when you're spending time there:

What is you favorite memory to share with people:

Write about the most amazing thing your body does or helps you do:

Think of the type of environments (City,
beach, mountains, etc.)that make you feel
alive and inspired and write about it:

Think about a person you believe gives the best advice to you all the time. And write about your feelings towards that person:

Think about your strongest skills. Write about how those skills help you make the world a better place:

_____

_____

_____

_____

_____

_____

_____

_____

_____

_____

_____

_____

_____

_____

_____

_____

_____

_____

Write about your personality trait that you're most proud of:

_____

_____

_____

_____

_____

_____

_____

_____

_____

_____

_____

_____

_____

_____

_____

_____

_____

_____

Think of something nice someone else has done for you lately. And describe how it made you feel:

_____

_____

_____

_____

_____

_____

_____

_____

_____

_____

_____

_____

_____

_____

_____

_____

_____

_____

_____

Think of something you have (doesn't have to be physical things) today but you didn't have a few years ago. And write about it:

Write about one thing you've learned lately. It can be anything!:

Write about the time when you feel most rested:

Think of a person (can be anybody) and write an imaginary conversation with that person. What would you tell?:

List 3 places you've visited last year that helped you to explore things around you:

_____

_____

_____

_____

_____

_____

_____

_____

_____

_____

_____

_____

_____

_____

_____

_____

_____

_____

Write about something (a time) you don't ever want to forget:

_____

_____

_____

_____

_____

_____

_____

_____

_____

_____

_____

_____

_____

_____

_____

_____

_____

_____

Write what you'd say to yourself at age 10 or 20 (or any other age), if you could go back in time:

_____

_____

_____

_____

_____

_____

_____

_____

_____

_____

_____

_____

_____

_____

_____

_____

_____

_____

_____

Think about a time period you'd like to be in
if you could go back in time. List the
reason why you'd choose that period:

Make a list of things you'd like to say yes to if you're ever given the opportunity to do so:

Think of 3 negative things you say about yourself and replace them with positive things:

Challenge yourself to replace negative scripts of your mind with positive words:

_____

_____

_____

_____

_____

_____

_____

_____

_____

_____

_____

_____

_____

_____

_____

_____

_____

Name a few things you can start doing next
week to take better care of yourself:

_____

_____

_____

_____

_____

_____

_____

_____

_____

_____

_____

_____

_____

_____

_____

Think of 5 reasons that make you a good friend:

_____

_____

_____

_____

_____

_____

_____

_____

_____

_____

_____

_____

_____

_____

_____

_____

_____

Write about the best dream you've ever had:

Write about something you've done lately but you didn't get to brag about. Use this space to brag about it:

_____

_____

_____

_____

_____

_____

_____

_____

_____

_____

_____

_____

_____

_____

_____

_____

_____

_____

Write when you feel the most confident.
Think if you can multiply those moments:

Write about the qualities you think others admire about you:

Write about what makes you happiest in life:

_____

_____

_____

_____

_____

_____

_____

_____

_____

_____

_____

_____

_____

_____

_____

_____

_____

_____

Set 3 short term goals and 3 long term
goals for yourself:

Write what your ultimate goal is in your life:

Write about what you've learned from this journaling experience:

Fill in these last pages with hope and positive things in your life. Let your worries go...

Fill in these last pages with hope and positive things in your life. Let your worries go...

Fill in these last pages with hope and positive things in your life. Let your worries go...

Fill in these last pages with hope and positive things in your life. Let your worries go...

Fill in these last pages with hope and
positive things in your life. Let your
worries go...

_____

_____

_____

_____

_____

_____

_____

_____

_____

_____

_____

_____

_____

_____

_____

_____

_____

Fill in these last pages with hope and positive things in your life. Let your worries go...

Fill in these last pages with hope and positive things in your life. Let your worries go...

Fill in these last pages with hope and positive things in your life. Let your worries go...

Fill in these last pages with hope and positive things in your life. Let your worries go...

Fill in these last pages with hope and positive things in your life. Let your worries go...

Fill in these last pages with hope and
positive things in your life. Let your
worries go...

_____

_____

_____

_____

_____

_____

_____

_____

_____

_____

_____

_____

_____

_____

_____

_____

_____

Fill in these last pages with hope and
positive things in your life. Let your
worries go...

Fill in these last pages with hope and positive things in your life. Let your worries go...

Fill in these last pages with hope and positive things in your life. Let your worries go...

Fill in these last pages with hope and positive things in your life. Let your worries go...

Fill in these last pages with hope and positive things in your life. Let your worries go...

Fill in these last pages with hope and positive things in your life. Let your worries go...

Fill in these last pages with hope and
positive things in your life. Let your
worries go...

Fill in these last pages with hope and
positive things in your life. Let your
worries go...

_____

_____

_____

_____

_____

_____

_____

_____

_____

_____

_____

_____

_____

_____

_____

_____

_____

_____

_____

Fill in these last pages with hope and positive things in your life. Let your worries go...

43616017R00070

Made in the USA
Lexington, KY
30 June 2019